GHOSTED?

WHY PEOPLE DISAPPEAR –
AND WHAT THEIR SILENCE
REALLY MEANS

BY PHIL TURNER JR.

Philio Publishing
www.philiopublishing.com

First Edition — 2026

ISBN: 978-0-9964356-1-1

Printed in the United States of America

Philio
P U B L I S H I N G

Disclaimer

The content in this book is intended for personal insight, emotional clarity, and educational purposes only. It is not a substitute for professional mental-health services, counseling, therapy, legal advice, or medical guidance.

While this book explores psychological patterns, emotional behaviors, and human tendencies, every person and every situation is unique. Results may vary based on individual circumstances, personal history, and emotional readiness.

The author does not make guarantees that reading this book will repair a relationship, prevent ghosting, or change the behavior of others. What this book *can* offer is a clearer understanding of human behavior, tools for emotional resilience, and a framework for healthier connections moving forward.

If you are experiencing emotional distress, trauma, or unsafe circumstances, please seek qualified professional support. Your wellbeing matters.

DEDICATION

To everyone whoever wondered,

"What happened?"

To the ones who gave their best only to be met with silence…

To those who cared deeply, trusted too soon, or loved too hard…

And to anyone who has ever been confused, blindsided, or left without closure

***

this book is for you.

And to the memory of my beloved wife, **Theresa L. Turner** —
your strength, compassion, and love continue to guide my purpose.

I also could not have found the strength to complete this book without the support of my friends and family — especially Ronald, Elona, Helen, Brandon, Yvette, Bonnie, TC, Little Bit, Brandi, Nise (Wanda), Elvin, Marsha, Khadijah, Ursula, Holly, Dee, my cousins, nieces and nephews, and my children — who constantly reached out, kept me focused, encouraged, and surrounded me with kindness during one of the most difficult seasons of my life.

AUTHOR'S NOTE

My life changed in ways I never expected in late 2024 and early 2025. I know what it feels like to lose someone you love — not just at the end, but slowly, through distance, silence, and the kind of emotional disconnect you can't stop no matter how hard you try.

Losing my wife, Theresa, didn't just break my heart. It reshaped the way I understand connection, vulnerability, and how fragile people can become when life hits them deeply.

That experience taught me something:

- People don't always disappear because they're careless or cruel.
- Sometimes they're overwhelmed, emotionally exhausted, or fighting invisible battles.
- Sometimes they retreat because life has already drained the part of them that knows how to stay.

I carry the memory of my wife, **Theresa L. Turner**, with love and gratitude. Her life remains a reminder of compassion, strength, and grace.

This is not a book about grief. But my journey taught me how easily people can vanish while still standing right in front of you — and how important it is to handle each other gently. That's why this book is written in a short, direct style: clarity hits harder than long explanations, and some truths don't need many words.

ABOUT ME

I'm Phil Turner Jr.—a Certified Strategic Interventionist, a Certified Relationship Coach, and a lifelong student of human behavior. My work in relationships began back in the late **1980s**, long before social media, dating apps, and modern communication patterns reshaped how people connect and disconnect.

Between **2008 and 2014**, I published several relationship books exploring dating, communication, self-awareness, and why people step back, shut down, or walk away from relationships. Those books led to years of coaching women and men who wanted clarity, confidence, and direction in their emotional lives.

And then—I stepped back.

Not because the work stopped mattering, but because the world changed.
A lot.

Over the last decade, completely new dynamics have shaped human relationships: constant texting, ghosting, emotional burnout, attachment styles going mainstream, social media validation loops, and an overwhelming amount of relationship content online. I wanted to understand these new variables without distraction or rushing to publish.

So, for **more than 13 years**, I coached quietly—mostly friends, friends of friends, and private referrals—while studying the shifts in human behavior up close. I listened. I observed. I watched patterns form and repeat. I saw people connect quickly and disconnect even faster. I studied ghosting long before the term became universal.

During this time, I deepened my training. My background includes:

- **Certified Strategic Interventionist (Robbins-Madanes Method)**
- **Certified Relationship Coach**
- Training in **Neuro-Linguistic Programming (NLP)**
- **Human Needs Psychology**
- Marriage education based on **Gottman Institute principles**
- Study of **Matrix Therapies**, emotional pattern techniques, conflict-resolution strategies, and relationship communication models

Although college educated, I am **not** a licensed therapist, psychologist, or clinical behaviorist—and I make that clear.

My strength comes from a combination of:

- decades of observation,
- real-world coaching,

- formal training in relationship-based methodologies,
- and lived human experience.

I've lived love, loss, connection, heartbreak, rebuilding, and deep personal growth. All of it shaped how I understand people. All of it shows up in my work.

While watching relationship content explode on YouTube and social media, I noticed something important: many modern creators focus on surface-level reactions, viral moments, and algorithm-safe topics. They avoid deeper truths to prevent strikes, backlash, or controversy. The problem is that surface-level advice cannot explain the emotional complexity behind why people disappear.

Something deeper has been missing. A vacuum needed to be filled.

That's why I returned.

Ghosted? is not a rehash of my early books. It is a modern, updated exploration built on years of quiet observation—watching how people respond to stress, fear, emotional overload, uncertainty, insecurity, and unmet expectations. This book was created to give you the clarity people rarely receive when someone exits their life in silence.

I don't claim perfection, and I don't pretend to have all the answers.

But I do have decades of study, experience, pattern recognition, and human insight.

If you're reading this, you're searching for understanding, peace, and emotional clarity.

And I'm honored to help you find it.

TABLE OF CONTENTS

INTRODUCTION

The Silent Exit

Ghosting isn't new — but the *way* it happens today is.
The silence is louder.
The confusion is sharper.
And the emotional impact is deeper than most people are willing to admit.

It doesn't matter if the connection was romantic, platonic, professional, or spiritual. It doesn't matter if it lasted three days, three months, or three years.
It doesn't matter whether you were "talking," "dating," "friends," "co-workers," "situationship-ing," or "almost something."

When someone disappears without warning —
when the calls stop…
when the messages slow down…
when the energy shifts…
when the warmth turns cold…
when the door quietly closes —

it hurts.
It confuses.
And it leaves you replaying every detail in your mind.

You start asking yourself the questions people rarely say out loud:

- *Did I miss a sign?*
- *Did I do something wrong?*
- *Did they get bored?*
- *Was I too much? Not enough? Too vulnerable? Not vulnerable enough?*
- *Did something happen—or did they just stop caring?*
- *And why didn't they just say something?*

Ghosting is modern rejection wrapped in silence.
It's a shutdown, a pullback, a slow fade, or a complete disappearance…
and it leaves the human mind searching for meaning.

But here's the truth no one tells you:

Ghosting almost never means what you think it means.

And it rarely has anything to do with your worth.
Most of the time, it's about:

- **their emotional capacity, not your value**
- **their fears, not your flaws**
- **their unresolved past, not your present behavior**
- **their worldview, not your character**
- **their discomfort, not your desirability**

Ghosting is a behavioral response, not a moral judgment. This book exists to help you understand that response — not just in dating, but in **all human relationships**:

- romantic partners
- friends
- co-workers
- neighbors
- situationships
- almost-relationships
- "we're talking but not sure what this is" connections
- business dealings
- mentorships
- family dynamics

Anyone can ghost.
Anyone can get ghosted.
And everyone has experienced the confusion that silence brings.

Why I Wrote This Book

Years ago, I wrote a book called *Why He Bounced*. It focused on men, dating, and the reasons men quietly walked away.
It helped thousands of women understand the "silent exit" from the male perspective.

But the world has changed dramatically since then.

- Dating has changed.
- Expectations have changed.
- Communication has changed.

- People have changed.
- The emotional bandwidth of this generation has changed.
- Even the *way* we avoid discomfort has changed.

Ghosting is no longer a dating problem — it is a human behavior problem.

And after 30 years of coaching, observing patterns, studying psychology, and guiding people behind the scenes... it became clear that ghosting deserved an updated conversation — one that is deeper, fairer, and fully modern.

Not just:

Why he ghosted.

Not just:

Why she ghosted.

But:

Why *they* ghosted — any "they," in any situation.

This book is not about blame. It's about understanding.

Why Ghosting Hits So Hard

Ghosting is painful because humans are wired for:

- **connection**
- **closure**
- **clarity**

And ghosting gives you none of the three.

It leaves you with unanswered questions and unresolved emotion — a mix that the brain hates because humans crave narrative.

Our minds don't just want to know what happened… they want to know *why*.

This book gives you the "why."

What You Will Learn

Across these pages, you'll discover:

- the real emotional, psychological, and behavioral reasons people disappear
- how fear, shame, projection, and overwhelm drive avoidance
- how trauma, insecurity, and identity influence ghosting
- how chemistry and biology change emotional availability

- the unspoken expectations that quietly sabotage connections
- the hidden pressures from friends, family, kids, money, religion, and culture
- the subtle behaviors that unintentionally push people away
- and the difference between:

  o someone who lost interest
  o someone who got scared
  o someone who felt unworthy
  o someone who was overwhelmed
  o someone who was emotionally unavailable
  o someone who was never serious
  o someone who cared but couldn't continue

You'll also learn how to become:

- more emotionally safe
- more self-aware
- more consistent
- more attractive in the ways that actually matter
- and more capable of building healthy, sustainable connection

You'll learn how to avoid ghosting patterns…
how to stop *attracting* people who disappear…
and how to protect your peace without shutting down emotionally.

This Is Not a Book About Blame

- This is a book about clarity.
- You deserve to understand what happened.
- You deserve to see the patterns clearly.
- You deserve to stop blaming yourself.
- You deserve the emotional freedom that comes when confusion finally ends.

And Here's the Most Important Truth

Ghosting says far more about **them** than it does about **you** —but it reveals something about *you*, too. You're about to learn what that is.

Welcome to a deeper understanding of human behavior. Welcome to the truth behind silence.

Welcome to **Ghosted**.

CHAPTER 1

DO PEOPLE EVEN KNOW WHAT THEY WANT?

BY PHIL TURNER JR.

Why Mixed Signals Lead to Disappearing Acts**

Before we can talk about ghosting — why it happens, how it happens, and what it means — we have to start with the most important truth:

Most people have no idea what they actually want.

Not in dating.
Not in relationships.
Not in friendships.
Not in business partnerships.
Not even in casual connections.

They *think* they know…
they *say* they know…
they may even convince themselves they know…
but when someone genuinely interested shows up, or when feelings get real, or when responsibility enters the picture — everything changes.

This confusion, inconsistency, and emotional unpreparedness is one of the **top reasons people ghost**.

- Ghosting isn't always rejection.
- Sometimes it's paralysis.
- Sometimes it's overwhelm.
- Sometimes it's self-protection.
- And sometimes it's avoidance because they don't know how to articulate their own truth.

Let's break down what this really looks like.

1. People Want Connection... Until Connection Requires Clarity

You've seen this pattern:

They want attention — but not accountability.
They want companionship — but not commitment.
They want intimacy — but not responsibility.
They want loyalty — but still want "options."
They want love — but they fear vulnerability.
They crave closeness — but panic when someone gets too close.

So what do they do?

They withdraw.
They pull back.
They fade out.
They ghost.
Not because you did anything wrong…

but because *clarity* requires emotional maturity — and many aren't ready for that.

2. People Confuse Interest With Impulse

Here's the truth:

- ✓ **Attraction is instant.**
- ✓ **Compatibility is evaluated.**
- ✓ **Readiness is chosen.**

Most people confuse the first two and never consider the third.

That's why you meet people who:

- feel excited on day one
- text nonstop for two weeks
- talk about "future plans"
- create emotional momentum
- *then disappear out of nowhere*

It wasn't fake.
It wasn't a lie.
It wasn't manipulation most of the time.

It was **impulse**, not **intention**.

And when the impulse cooled — they didn't have the emotional bandwidth to maintain the connection, nor the maturity to communicate honestly.

3. Most People Carry Unhealed Stories From Their Past

Ghosting often comes from:

- past heartbreak
- past rejection
- childhood wounds
- fear of abandonment
- fear of intimacy

- fear of conflict
- fear of disappointing someone
- fear of being "exposed"
- fear of repeating a painful pattern

When the past gets triggered, they don't run — they vanish.

It's easier to disappear than to explain something they don't even understand within themselves.

4. Many People Want Love, But Not the Work of Love

Everyone wants the feelings:
the romance, the fun, the attention, the high, the connection.

But very few want:

- the communication
- the emotional consistency
- the sacrifice
- the compromise
- the accountability
- the patience
- the vulnerability
- the truth
- the maturity
- the growth

So when love stops being *easy* and starts being *real* —
they check out silently.

**Ghosting is often the exit door for people who want
the experience, not the responsibility.**

5. People Don't Understand Their Own Emotional Capacity

A person can like you…
find you attractive…
enjoy talking to you…
and even feel connected to you…

…and still not have the emotional capacity for what
you want.

Capacity determines everything:

- their ability to stay consistent
- their ability to respond
- their ability to communicate
- their ability to show up
- their ability to be honest
- their ability to handle complexity

Ghosting happens when their **capacity** doesn't match
your **connection**.

6. People Don't Understand the Weight of Their Words

These days, "future talk" is recreational.
People casually say:

- "I can see us going far."
- "I'm not going anywhere."
- "You're different."
- "I want something real."
- "I'm ready for a relationship."

…but the words are powered by emotion, not intention. And when reality doesn't match the fantasy they created — they disappear.

Ghosting is the escape from accountability for promises made too quickly.

7. People Want Assurance Without Offering Assurance

Most people want:

- exclusivity
- security
- priority
- consistency
- reassurance

…but they don't give the same in return.

And when they realize a real connection requires reciprocity — they ghost because it feels like too much pressure.

8. This Generation Is Overstimulated and Underskilled

This isn't about age — it's about culture.
People today are:

- emotionally overloaded
- socially exhausted
- mentally overwhelmed
- overstimulated by technology
- desensitized to human connection
- unfamiliar with healthy communication
- experts at avoiding discomfort

This is the perfect storm for ghosting.

Most people were never taught:

- how to end a conversation respectfully
- how to say "I'm not ready"
- how to say "I'm interested but overwhelmed"
- how to say "I like you but can't continue"
- how to set boundaries
- how to give closure

So they do the only thing they know:
avoid.

9. Many Don't Know the Difference Between Compatibility and Chemistry

Chemistry creates excitement.
Compatibility creates sustainability.

People chase the first and run from the second.

Ghosting often happens when:

- the high wears off
- the dopamine drops
- the reality settles in
- the connection requires depth
- the true personalities emerge

They disappear because chemistry excited them — but compatibility challenged them.

10. And Finally... People Ghost Because Silence Feels Easier Than Truth

Not kinder.
Not better.
Not respectful.

Just *easier*.

People ghost because silence gives them:

- no confrontation
- no explanation

- no accountability
- no discomfort
- no emotional labor
- no responsibility

It's a short-term relief for them…
and a long-term confusion for you.

The Takeaway

Ghosting reflects **their emotional state**, not your value.

Before you take it personally…
before you blame yourself…
before you assume you "did something wrong"…

remember this:

Most people are not ready for the connection they say they want — and ghosting is the symptom of that unpreparedness.

In the next chapters, we'll break down the psychology, patterns, reasons, and red flags — and most importantly, how to never internalize someone's disappearance again.

CHAPTER 2

SIGNS THEY WERE
NEVER READY
(EVEN IF THEY THOUGHT
THEY WERE)

Why Ghosting Often Starts Long Before the Disappearance

Before ghosting ever happens, there are always **early indicators** — signs that a person is emotionally unprepared, unavailable, or unstable in ways that *you didn't recognize at the time.*

Ghosting doesn't begin the day someone stops texting. It begins the moment they show you they don't have the clarity, capacity, or consistency required for a real connection.

This chapter lays out the **most common signs someone was never ready** — whether the connection was romantic, friendly, professional, or a situationship that felt like something more.

1. Inconsistent Communication From Day One

People show you who they are through patterns, not promises.

Early inconsistency is one of the biggest indicators of someone who will eventually ghost. These patterns include:

- texting all day Monday, disappearing Tuesday
- talking deep one week and cold the next
- showing excitement in person but flat energy online

- sharing affection but not following through
- making plans but canceling repeatedly

It's not the inconsistency that hurts — it's the meaning behind it:

Their emotions fluctuate. Their availability fluctuates. Their interest fluctuates.
And ultimately… their presence fluctuates.

This is not someone who is ready for connection.

2. They Wanted Intimacy Without Emotional Responsibility

A person who wants:

- compliments,
- affection,
- emotional access,
- your time,
- your attention,
- your energy…

…but avoids accountability for how their behavior affects you — is not ready.

This applies to:

- friends who vent but never show up for you
- coworkers who lean on you but don't support you

- romantic interests who want closeness but not commitment

They wanted what felt good…
not what was required.

3. They Never Made Things Clear

Ghosting thrives in ambiguity.

Someone who's not ready often communicates in fog:

- "I'm not sure what I want right now."
- "Let's just see where it goes."
- "I'm not good at relationships but I like you."
- "I'm not ready for anything serious, but I don't want to lose you."
- "I need space, but I don't want distance."

Translation?
They want the benefits of connection without the vulnerability of clarity.

And when clarity becomes necessary — they disappear.

4. They Were Emotionally Guarded to the Point of Inaccessibility

Some guard their heart; others barricade it.

Examples:

- they would open up, but only at surface level
- they avoided deeper conversations
- they got uncomfortable when you asked emotional questions
- they never talked about feelings
- they shut down when things got serious
- they changed the subject when vulnerability approached

Emotionally unavailable people don't ghost because of *you* —
they ghost because anything real feels threatening.

5. Their Life Was in Chaos — But They Called It "Just a Phase"

Ghosting often comes from emotional overload, not rejection.

Signs include:

- going through a fresh breakup
- dealing with unresolved trauma
- mental health challenges
- unstable living situation
- job stress or financial collapse
- ongoing conflict with an ex
- trying to "find themselves"

- family turmoil
- any kind of identity crisis

People in chaos rarely have the space for consistency. They bond quickly, detach quickly, and ghost easily.

6. Their Past Still Had a Grip on Them

Unhealed wounds always resurface.
People who ghost often carry:

- trust issues
- abandonment fears
- trauma bonds
- attachment triggers
- emotional numbness
- fear of repeating past pain
- guilt from previous relationships
- resentment from being hurt

They were never ready — not because they didn't like you, but because they never healed.

7. They Had Too Many Open Doors From Their Past

This is one of the biggest reasons someone ghosts:

They never closed the doors behind them.

Examples:

- the ex still calls
- they still "talk" to past partners
- they have flirtationships lingering
- their "friend circle" is full of former lovers
- they keep people around for ego boosts
- they use attention as currency

If their past is crowded, their future with you will be temporary.

People don't ghost when they're fully available —
they ghost when they're emotionally divided.

8. They Wanted Validation More Than Connection

If someone liked how you made them feel more than they liked *you*, they were never ready.

People craving validation:

- disappear when the high fades
- ghost when attention shifts
- pull back when admiration isn't constant
- lose interest when you stop feeding their ego

You didn't do anything wrong —
you just stopped being their emotional charger.

9. Their Words and Actions Didn't Match

One of the clearest signs someone will ghost:

They spoke like they wanted depth but behaved like they wanted convenience.

Examples:

- they talked about "future plans" but never followed through
- they said "I miss you" but never saw you
- they said "I'm serious about this" while acting casual
- they said "you're important to me" but didn't prioritize you
- they acted relationship-ish but denied the relationship

Ghosting becomes the "escape hatch" when the illusion collapses.

10. They Struggled With Direct Communication

People who can't communicate simple truths —
will definitely struggle with uncomfortable ones.

Signs include:

- avoiding conflict
- shutting down when things feel heavy
- apologizing without changing behavior
- giving half-answers
- going quiet after disagreements
- needing days to "reset" after emotional moments
- avoiding confrontation at all costs

Ghosting is the ultimate conflict-avoidance behavior.

If they couldn't handle small tension...
they definitely couldn't handle emotional truth.

11. They Were Not Ready for Your Intensity, Depth, or Expectations

Sometimes ghosting happens because **you were ready — and they weren't.**

You brought:

- clarity
- consistency
- communication
- emotional maturity
- honesty
- effort
- accountability
- real interest

They brought:

- confusion
- half-effort
- mixed signals
- inconsistent availability
- emotional immaturity

They didn't ghost because you were "too much."
They ghosted because they were **too little** for what you required.

12. They Were Looking for a Feeling, Not a Foundation

This is one of the deepest truths in modern relationships: **People want the spark, not the structure.**

They want:

- butterflies
- excitement
- dopamine
- attention
- novelty
- thrill

But they don't want:

- routine
- accountability

- emotional depth
- real conversations
- adjustments
- expectations

So when the spark settles into something real —
they ghost because they don't know how to transition
from *feeling* to *building*.

FINAL THOUGHT FOR CHAPTER 2

Ghosting says far more about their preparedness than
your worth.

Most people don't disappear because something is wrong
with you…
they disappear because something is unresolved within
themselves.

Your job is not to fix their readiness.
Your job is to recognize the signs *before* you invest your
heart.

CHAPTER 3

WHY THEY PULLED BACK: THE PSYCHOLOGY BEHIND EMOTIONAL RETREAT

Ghosting doesn't always come from a place of cruelty or indifference.

Sometimes it's fear.

Sometimes it's shame.

Sometimes it's confusion.

Sometimes it's self-protection.

And sometimes it's simply a person hitting their emotional limit.

This chapter breaks down the *core psychological drivers* behind why people retreat, even when everything seemed to be going well.

1. Emotional Overload: When Connection Feels Like Too Much

Some people shut down when emotions rise beyond their comfort zone.

This happens when:

- they've been hurt before
- they fear abandonment
- vulnerability feels dangerous
- affection triggers old memories
- they're used to instability
- they have unhealed trauma
- they simply don't know how to receive care

Pulling back becomes their way of "regulating" themselves — but it ends up hurting you.

To them, it's survival.
To you, it's confusion.

2. Fear of Rejection: Better to Disappear Than Be Denied

Many people fear being rejected more than they fear losing the connection.

They think:
"If I stay, I might get hurt; if I pull back, I control the outcome."

Signs this fear is driving them:

- they keep you at arm's length
- they only open up in small doses
- they seem unsure even when things are going well
- they try to stay "detached"
- they react strongly to small misunderstandings
- they avoid conversations about the future

Ghosting, in their mind, is a way to avoid the pain they've already imagined.

3. Feeling Not Good Enough (Deep Insecurity They'll Never Admit)

A truth many people never say out loud:

Some ghost because they don't feel they deserve you.

Their inner thoughts may sound like:

- "They're too good for me."
- "I can't give them what they need."
- "I'm not ready for someone like them."
- "What if they see my flaws and walk away?"

So instead of opening up... they disappear.

Not because you weren't valuable —
but because they didn't believe *they* were valuable enough.

4. Anxiety Around Expectations

Some people can't handle expectations — even normal, healthy ones.

Examples:

- consistent communication
- emotional reciprocity
- being present
- showing effort
- making plans
- being honest

Even the *idea* of needing to show up creates anxiety.

So they retreat before expectations rise.

They're not rejecting *you* —
they're rejecting the responsibility of connection.

5. Their Nervous System Doesn't Know Peace

This is especially common in people raised around chaos, instability, or unpredictable environments.

To them:

- kindness feels suspicious
- stability feels unfamiliar
- consistency feels overwhelming
- affection feels too intense
- healthy love feels unsafe

So they sabotage or retreat because peace feels like a setup.

If someone has only known survival, comfort will confuse them.

6. They're Afraid of Hurting You (Even Though Ghosting Hurts More)

Some people retreat when they feel their interest shifting or fading.

Not because they don't care...
but because they **don't know how to communicate decline** without feeling guilty.

Their logic (wrong but common):

- "If I pull back slowly, it'll hurt less."
- "If I fade out, maybe they'll lose interest too."
- "If I don't say it out loud, I'm not the villain."

They ghost to avoid the heaviness of truth.

7. They're Comparing You to Someone From Their Past

This isn't fair — but it's real.

Sometimes they pull back because:

- a past partner hurt them
- a previous relationship ended unexpectedly
- they're still healing
- they still have emotional ties elsewhere
- they're afraid of repeating old patterns

You triggered something familiar...
and instead of handling it, they withdrew.

8. They Wanted You Until You Wanted Them Back

The oldest dynamic in modern dating:

Some people chase the feeling of being wanted, not the relationship itself.

When you reciprocate:

- the chase ends
- the mystery dissolves
- the fear of responsibility rises
- they lose interest
- they retreat

They confuse attachment with attraction.
And when the "high" wears off… they pull back.

9. Your Vulnerability Triggered Their Avoidant Side

Attachment styles play a huge role in pullback behavior.

Avoidant individuals get overwhelmed by:

- closeness
- feelings
- connection
- emotional expression
- needs
- intimacy

When things get too real, too soon — they retreat to re-establish distance and control.

Your vulnerability didn't push them away.
Their discomfort with intimacy did.

10. They Saw Red Flags in Themselves, Not in You

People who are self-aware (but not self-healed) will sometimes pull away because they know:

- they're inconsistent
- they're not stable
- they're unreliable
- they're unhealed
- they're emotionally unavailable
- they're not ready for a good person

Instead of rising to the occasion — they step back.

Not because you were wrong…
but because they were.

11. They Felt the Connection Getting Real

The human mind does something interesting:

When something feels meaningful, it also feels risky.

Signs the connection was getting real for *them*:

- deeper conversations
- growing attachment
- emotional safety
- increasing closeness
- them opening up
- you becoming important

For someone who's not ready —
that realization is terrifying.

And instead of leaning in… they retreat.

12. They Don't Know How to Regulate Emotionally After Intimacy

For many people, closeness activates old wounds.

After sex or deep connection, they may feel:

- exposed
- vulnerable
- overwhelmed
- attached too quickly
- emotionally naked
- scared they care too much

So they pull back, not because the moment was bad —
but because it was powerful.

13. They Retreat Because You Saw Them Too Clearly

Some people are uncomfortable being seen.

Truly seen.

Your presence may have:

- reflected their flaws
- highlighted their insecurities
- challenged their patterns
- exposed their inconsistency
- raised their standards

When you become a mirror...some run.

FINAL THOUGHT FOR CHAPTER 3

Pullback is rarely random.
It's rarely sudden.
And it's almost never about you.

People retreat when the connection:

- triggers fear
- demands growth
- exposes insecurity
- challenges patterns
- requires effort they can't give
- brings up emotions they don't know how to manage

Understanding these psychological roots doesn't excuse the behavior —
but it does help you stop internalizing it.

They didn't pull back because you weren't enough. They pulled back because connection asked for more than they had to give.

CHAPTER 4

**ARE YOU READY FOR LOVE?

Emotional Availability, Self-Sabotage & The Signals You Don't Realize You're Sending**

Before we talk about why someone ghosted *you*, we need to look at something harder:

Were you actually ready for the connection you wanted?

Ghosting isn't always about the other person.
Sometimes people disappear because they walk into a situation that feels emotionally unavailable, messy, confusing, or unstable — even when you didn't intend it.

Chapter 4 is about the mirror.

Not for blame. For clarity.

1. Emotional Availability: Are You Truly Open or Just "Wanting Something Different"?

People often say they want a serious relationship…

…but their habits say:

- "I'm exhausted."
- "I'm scared."
- "I'm not healed yet."
- "I want connection without vulnerability."
- "I want love, but only on my terms."

Signs **you may not be as ready as you think**:

- You still compare new people to past partners
- You hold on to old emotional attachments
- You fear rejection more than you desire connection
- You sabotage when things feel peaceful
- You struggle to trust consistency
- You overanalyze small things
- You expect people to prove they won't leave

Ghosting often happens when someone picks up on your internal conflict.

Because emotional ambiguity is felt before it is spoken.

2. Are You Still Entertaining "Past Men/Women You Call Friends"?

This is one of the biggest reasons high-quality men and women quietly back away.

If you:

- still text old partners
- still answer calls from exes
- still keep "friendships" with situationships
- still keep men or women around for ego boosts
- still have emotional residue from your past
- still have your past showing up in your phone, inbox, or DMs

…it sends a loud message:

"I'm not finished with the past, but I want you to invest in my future."

No relationship-worthy person wants to compete with ghosts of your past.

And yes — people DO check:

- your IG
- your comments
- your pictures
- who you follow
- your call history (if they ever accidentally see it)
- what kinds of people engage with you

Not because they're insecure —
but because they don't want to walk into a battlefield they didn't sign up for.

3. Ego Attachments: When You Keep Past People Around Because It Feels Good

Some people don't realize how much emotional noise they create by holding onto:

- old situations
- flirtation friendships
- "just checking on you" exes

- men or women who won't go away
- people who once had access and still feel entitled

Ask yourself honestly:

Do these people serve your future or just your ego?

If they disappeared tomorrow, would anything meaningful be lost?

If the answer is no —
that's your sign.

People ghost when they sense your heart is crowded.

4. Are You Presentable Emotionally, Mentally, and Spiritually?

Men and women who are ready for real connection look for signs you can:

- handle conflict
- take accountability
- manage your emotions
- communicate directly
- show respect
- show gratitude
- receive affection without suspicion
- create peace, not chaos

If you:

- overreact
- assume the worst
- snap easily
- lead with negativity
- live in survival mode
- are still angry from old relationships
- are guarded and unavailable

People don't ghost you because you're unworthy.

They ghost because interacting with you feels unsafe to *them*.

Emotional volatility scares people away quietly.

5. The Energy You Carry Will Tell Them Everything

Are you showing up as:

- **bitter or healed?**
- **hopeful or guarded?**
- **peaceful or chaotic?**
- **present or stuck in the past?**
- **appreciative or entitled?**
- **curious or suspicious?**

Energy is the first language of relationships.

People sense when something is "off" long before they can explain it.

If your energy says:

- "I'm guarded"
- "I'm unavailable"
- "I've been hurt and I'm looking for signs you'll hurt me too"
- "I'm tired and hoping love will fix it"
- "I'll sabotage the minute I feel threatened"

…it doesn't matter how attractive, smart, or accomplished you are.

People retreat from emotional weight.

6. When Your Life Is Too Crowded for Love

You can't build a new relationship in a life that has:

- too much chaos
- too many unresolved situations
- too many emotional obligations
- too many friends influencing you
- too many distractions
- too little peace

People ghost when they sense you don't have the space for them.

Not physical space — emotional bandwidth.

If you're:

- always busy
- always drained
- always stressed
- always overwhelmed
- always in crisis mode

…then you may want love, but you're not ready to sustain it.

7. Emotional Availability Checklist

Be honest:

Do you still feel connected to past partners?

- Do you allow exes to call or check in?
- Do men or women you used to date still contact you?
- Do you have someone you keep around for attention?
- Do you compare new people to old relationships?
- Are you afraid to trust someone new?
- Are you emotionally exhausted?
- Are you hoping someone else will fix your loneliness?
- Do you keep "options" just in case?
- Are you truly ready for someone to choose you?

If you answered **yes** to several…
you aren't ready for the connection you're hoping for — yet.

Not because something is wrong with you.
Because healing and readiness take time.

8. When People Ghost Because You Weren't Ready — Even If You Didn't Know It

People who are healthy, emotionally grounded, and relationship-worthy can feel when:

- your past is still active
- your heart is still fragile
- your energy is conflicted
- your boundaries are unclear
- your world is loud
- your emotions are unstable
- your life is too crowded
- you're craving companionship, not connection

They may never say it.
They'll just step back.

Ghosting doesn't always mean rejection.
Sometimes it's them saying:
"You're not ready for the kind of connection I want."

CLOSING THOUGHT FOR CHAPTER 4

This chapter is not about blame — it's about readiness.

Before someone invests in you, they're reading your emotional world.

People don't just ghost because of who *they* are.
They ghost because of what they *sense* in you.

And when you get honest about your readiness,
you stop internalizing ghosting as a personal failure —
and start seeing it as an invitation to align your heart,
your habits, and your emotional environment.

CHAPTER 5

**MIXED SIGNALS & EMOTIONAL MATH:

How People Interpret Your Actions (Even When You Don't Mean It)**

No one ghosts without a story forming in their mind first.

And that story — right or wrong — usually comes from the **signals you never realized you were sending**.

Humans are emotional mathematicians.
We add up:

- tone
- timing
- consistency
- effort
- hesitation
- body language
- social media behavior
- responsiveness
- boundaries
- contradictions
- facial expressions

…and we try to solve one equation:

"Is this person safe for me to connect with?"

Chapter 5 explores how people interpret your signals, even when you meant nothing by them.

1. The Silent Language of Consistency

People don't need perfection —
they need **predictability**.

When someone senses:

- your energy shifts
- you're hot one day and cold the next
- you respond quickly one moment, then disappear another
- you're affectionate in private but guarded in public
- you talk about wanting connection but act unavailable

…it creates confusion.

And confusion is the #1 trigger for ghosting.

People don't ghost because they're cruel.
They ghost because:

"I can't tell where this is going."
"I don't know what they want."
"Something feels off but I can't explain it."

Consistency is not about frequency —
it's about reliability.

2. When Your Words Say One Thing, But Your Behavior Says Another

Mixed signals come in many forms:

- Saying "I'm looking for something serious"
- while entertaining people who don't want commitment.
- Saying "I'm over my ex"
- while posting breakup quotes.
- Saying "I value honesty"
- while withholding information out of fear.
- Saying "I'm easygoing"
- while creating tension over small things.

Mixed signals don't require bad intentions —
they just require contradiction.

And most people won't stick around long enough for clarification.

3. Emotional Inflation vs. Emotional Deflation

Some people unintentionally **inflate** emotions early:

- long calls
- long texts
- intimate conversations
- deep vulnerability
- future talk

- nonstop compliments
- quick attachment

Then suddenly deflate:

- fewer calls
- shorter texts
- less energy
- less enthusiasm
- less responsiveness
- less intimacy

This emotional whiplash is often interpreted as:

- manipulation
- insincerity
- loss of interest
- conflicting priorities
- emotional instability

Even if none of that is true.

Ghosting becomes the exit when the emotional math feels dangerous.

4. Over-Sharing vs. Under-Sharing

Oversharing (trauma dumping, too many details, too soon) makes people feel overwhelmed.

Undersharing (vague, closed off, guarded)
makes people feel they're hitting a wall.

Both extremes create discomfort.
Healthy connection requires a middle ground:

- honesty without intensity
- openness without flooding
- vulnerability without pressure

When that balance is missing, people retreat.

5. Looking for Red Flags Everywhere

Some people enter dating with:

- anxiety
- suspicion
- hypervigilance
- fear of repeating the past

So they look for:

- inconsistencies
- tone shifts
- slow replies
- harmless comments
- minor mistakes

…and label them as warning signs.

When someone feels "constantly evaluated," connection becomes exhausting.

They may quietly slip away because they feel judged instead of understood.

6. Social Media Signals

(You may not think they matter — but they do.)

People read into:

- who you follow
- who likes your posts
- what you comment on
- your selfies
- your outfits
- your memes
- your hidden relationships
- subliminal messages
- the energy of your online presence

A person with serious intentions is evaluating whether your online world matches the relationship energy you claim to want.

- If you say you want a committed partner but post thirst traps…
- If you claim you're healed but post bitterness…
- If you say you're private but overshare online…

People question the alignment.
And when there's doubt, ghosting becomes the exit.

7. Availability vs. Desperation

There is a difference between:

- being **available**
- and
- being **too available**.

When someone senses:

- you drop everything instantly
- you have no boundaries
- you respond instantly every time
- you change plans too easily
- you center your entire schedule around them

…it doesn't feel flattering.

It feels like pressure.

Healthy people want to earn connection —
not feel forced into it.

Ghosting often happens when interest feels unequal or rushed.

8. Emotional Pressure They Never Agreed To

Sometimes people ghost not because of you —
but because of the pressure they feel from what you *want*.

Pressure shows up when you:

- expect emotional commitments early
- assume exclusivity too soon
- read too much into early chemistry
- need constant reassurance
- expect deep intimacy without deep time
- want clarity before a foundation exists

People want connection —
but at a pace that feels safe.

When you move faster emotionally than they do,
ghosting becomes a shield.

9. The Misinterpretation Problem

You may think:

- "I'm being friendly."
- They think: you're flirting.

You may think:

- "I'm being direct."
- They think: you're aggressive.

You may think:

- "I'm just venting."
- They think: you're emotionally unstable.

You may think:

- "I'm being honest."
- They think: you're oversharing.

You may think:

- "I'm simply curious."
- They think: you're interrogating.

Intentions don't cancel impact.

Ghosting often happens because someone misread your signal —
and chose distance instead of conversation.

10. When People Can't Read You at All

The most ghosted people are often:

- mysterious
- vague
- guarded
- unpredictable
- emotionally inconsistent
- unclear about what they want
- afraid of vulnerability

It doesn't mean you're doing something wrong.

It means people can't **feel** you.

And when people don't feel you,
they don't invest.

Ghosting becomes a quiet release from uncertainty.

CLOSING THOUGHT FOR CHAPTER 5

Mixed signals are not always intentional.
Sometimes they're simply the side effect of:

- fear
- past trauma
- emotional exhaustion
- overthinking
- insecurity
- inexperience
- or trying too hard to "get it right."

But mixed signals are still signals.

People respond to what they *feel*, not what you *meant*.

When your emotional math doesn't add up for them,
ghosting becomes the easiest equation to solve.

CHAPTER 6

THE RULES OF GHOSTING (AND WHY PEOPLE DISAPPEAR WITHOUT WARNING)

Ghosting is not random.

It's not impulsive.

It's not immature behavior "just because."

Ghosting follows **patterns, instincts, triggers, and emotional logic** — even if that logic isn't fair.

Most people ghost for one of four reasons:

1. **Avoidance**
2. **Self-protection**
3. **Conflict aversion**
4. **Emotional overwhelm**

This chapter breaks down the "rules" — the unspoken mechanics — that lead to someone silently pulling away, disappearing, or going cold.

1. Ghosting Rule #1: People Avoid What They Don't Want to Confront

Ghosting is avoidance on autopilot.

People avoid:

- difficult conversations
- hurting someone's feelings
- explaining themselves
- being the bad guy
- conflict or pushback

- emotional intensity
- uncomfortable truth

Ghosting becomes:
"If I leave quietly, I don't have to face the discomfort."

It's wrong —
but it's real.

2. Ghosting Rule #2: People Ghost When Something Feels "Off," Even If They Can't Name It

Many disappearances happen because of a **feeling**, not a fact.

This includes:

- tone shifts
- vibe changes
- discomfort
- unresolved intuition
- subconscious patterns
- old wounds being activated

People rarely tell you:
"I don't know why, but something just doesn't sit right."

Instead, they vanish.

It's emotional instinct, not logic.

3. Ghosting Rule #3: People Ghost When the Relationship Becomes a "Mental Load" Instead of a Connection

If being around you feels like:

- work
- pressure
- emotional labor
- constant reassurance
- constant explaining
- confusion
- conflict
- fear of disappointing you

People retreat.

Ghosting becomes a way to **lighten their emotional load**, even at the cost of connection.

4. Ghosting Rule #4: People Ghost to Escape Responsibility

Not every ghoster is a villain —
but many are escaping responsibility.

Responsibility such as:

- telling you the truth
- admitting they lost interest
- respecting your feelings

- apologizing
- setting proper boundaries
- ending things like an adult

To them, ghosting feels like:
"If I say nothing, it becomes nothing."

5. Ghosting Rule #5: People Ghost When They Think You Will Try to Change Their Mind

Some disappear because they expect:

- persuasion
- tears
- anger
- negotiation
- guilt trips
- explanations
- emotional debates

They fear:
"If I try to end it respectfully, they'll make it harder."

So they disappear instead.

6. Ghosting Rule #6: People Ghost When They Feel Outmatched Emotionally

Not everyone can operate at your emotional level.

Some people bail because they feel:

- not enough
- not ready
- not healed
- not stable
- not capable
- not equipped

You may think you're being warm and honest.
They may feel pressure and expectation they cannot live up to.

Ghosting becomes a quiet surrender.

7. Ghosting Rule #7: People Ghost When They're Juggling Multiple Attachments

You are not always the only person they're talking to.

Ghosting often happens when:

- another connection becomes stronger
- someone from their past returns
- their situationship evolves
- they choose someone else
- they decide to commit elsewhere

Instead of explaining this shift,
they just disappear.

8. Ghosting Rule #8: People Ghost When They See a Serious Red Flag (or Believe They Do)

This can be:

- emotional instability
- disrespect
- guarded behavior
- jealousy
- controlling tendencies
- poor communication
- inconsistent boundaries
- excessive pressure
- unresolved ex drama

OR…

A red flag that isn't real —
simply a trigger from their past.

But ghosting still happens, because to them the red flag **felt real**.

9. Ghosting Rule #9: People Ghost When They Lose Interest but Don't Want to Look Like the Bad Guy

The hardest truth to swallow:

Sometimes they ghost because the spark faded.

Not because you're not valuable —

but because attraction is emotional wiring, not logic.

They don't want to say:

- "I don't feel the chemistry anymore."
- "I don't see a future with you."
- "It's not you, it's me."

So they escape through silence.

10. Ghosting Rule #10: People Ghost When They Realize They Can't Meet Your Needs

This one is rarely discussed.

Many disappear because:

- you want more than they can give
- you need more closeness than they can handle
- they are not ready for commitment
- they don't want a relationship
- they are not emotionally available
- they know they will disappoint you

Ghosting becomes "mercy avoidance":
a selfish act wrapped in a misguided belief that silence causes less harm.

11. Ghosting Rule #11: People Ghost When You Trigger Something They Haven't Healed

Ghosting is often the result of:

- past trauma
- abandonment wounds
- attachment issues
- unresolved childhood pain
- old relationships that ended badly

You didn't do anything wrong —
they just hit an internal wall.

And instead of dealing with it,
they shut down.

12. Ghosting Rule #12: People Ghost Because... They Can

Technology has made it easy.

There is no:

- accountability
- community pressure
- face-to-face confrontation
- loss of reputation

Ghosting is the **path of least resistance**.
And many take it.

13. Ghosting Rule #13: People Ghost to Preserve the Illusion of Being a "Good Person"

Ironically, they think silence protects their image.

They tell themselves:

- "If I explain, they'll think I'm a jerk."
- "If I distance slowly, that's kinder."
- "If I disappear, they can move on faster."

Of course, this is untrue —
but ghosting allows them to avoid looking in the mirror.

CLOSING THOUGHT FOR CHAPTER 6

Ghosting isn't personal — even when it feels painfully personal.

It's usually about:

- emotional comfort
- emotional avoidance
- emotional capacity
- emotional fear

Ghosting says more about *where someone is internally*
than anything they saw in you.

When someone disappears, remember:

Their silence is a reflection of their readiness — not your worth.

CHAPTER 7

THE AVOIDERS:
HOW CONFLICT-AVOIDANT
PEOPLE GHOST TO ESCAPE
DISCOMFORT

Not everyone ghosts because they're cruel.
Not everyone ghosts because they're selfish.
Some ghost because they truly **don't know how to stay** when things get real.

Avoidant personalities — emotionally avoidant, conflict avoidant, or intimacy avoidant — are the **runners** of the dating and relationship world.

They vanish for one core reason:

Discomfort feels like danger.
Closeness feels like pressure.
Accountability feels like conflict.

Ghosting becomes their safety exit.

This chapter unpacks *why* avoidant people disappear and how their patterns quietly show up long before the ghosting ever happens.

1. Why Avoidant People Ghost: The Three Hidden Fears

Avoidant individuals usually carry one or more of these deep emotional fears:

A. Fear of Being "Trapped"

They worry that:

- expectations will grow
- intimacy will require more from them
- you'll need emotional depth they can't sustain
- connection equals obligation

Ghosting becomes a premature escape from perceived captivity.

B. Fear of Confrontation

Avoidants hate:

- uncomfortable conversations
- explaining themselves
- disappointing someone
- being misunderstood
- emotional tension
- dealing with hurt feelings

So instead of saying:
"I don't think we're compatible,"
they disappear to dodge discomfort.

C. Fear of Emotional Exposure

Avoidants were often raised in environments where:

- vulnerability wasn't safe

- emotions were minimized
- independence was survival
- affection came with conditions

Connecting deeply feels dangerous.
Ghosting feels emotionally safer.

2. The Five Avoidant Archetypes (And How Each One Ghosts)

Not all avoidants ghost the same way.
Here are the most common patterns:

A. The Slow Fader

Their style:

- responses slow down
- calls get shorter
- plans become vague
- texts become inconsistent

They hope you'll "get the hint" so they won't have to say anything out loud.

B. The Vanisher

Everything is normal… until it isn't.

One day:

- great conversation

- great date
- great connection

Next day:
Silence. Nothing. Disappeared.

No argument.
No conflict.
Just emotional overwhelm.

C. The Exit Planner

This avoidant maps their exit before they disappear.

Signals include:

- emotionally checking out
- creating distance
- nitpicking
- becoming hyper-independent
- making excuses
- withholding affection

They're ghosting you *before* they physically ghost you.

D. The Polite Ghoster

This one believes they are doing you a kindness.

They tell themselves:

- "I'm sparing their feelings."
- "Disappearing is gentler than telling the truth."

- "If I fade quietly, they'll hurt less."

It's wrong — but their intention is not to harm.
It's to avoid guilt.

E. The Reappearing Ghost

This avoidant vanishes… but always returns.

Why?

Because disappearing wasn't about you.
It was about them feeling:

- overwhelmed
- stressed
- insecure
- inadequate
- unprepared

Once the pressure lifts, they pop back up as if nothing happened.

3. Avoidants Ghost When Things Start Feeling "Too Real"

Avoidants fear momentum.

This is where ghosting often begins:

- after intimacy
- after vulnerability

- after a meaningful conversation
- after a deep emotional moment
- after you express interest
- after they feel "too seen"

Closeness triggers their retreat instinct.

Ghosting becomes a pressure-release valve.

4. Avoidants Ghost When You Hit Their "Emotional Wall"

Avoidant individuals have unspoken limits:

- too many questions
- too much emotional need
- too much depth too soon
- too much consistency
- too much access

To them, this feels like:

- pressure
- expectation
- obligation
- loss of independence

So they hit the escape button.

5. Ghosting Works for Them — That's Why They Keep Doing It

Avoidants ghost because it:

- prevents confrontation
- avoids responsibility
- maintains their sense of control
- keeps emotional peace
- minimizes guilt
- protects their independence

Ghosting is their dysfunctional comfort zone.

6. How to Recognize an Avoidant Before They Ghost

Look for these signs:

- inconsistent communication
- unpredictable availability
- hot-cold behavior
- discomfort with intimacy
- keeps emotions surface-level
- avoids defining the relationship
- gets irritated by emotional needs
- prefers texting/DMs over calls
- disappears under stress
- struggles with accountability

These are **warning signals**, not judgments.
Avoidants aren't bad people — but they are risky partners if you need consistency.

7. Can You Make an Avoidant Stop Ghosting?

In short:
No — unless they want to change.

Avoidant behavior is:

- an attachment pattern
- a coping mechanism
- a learned emotional survival strategy

You cannot coach someone out of ghosting.
You cannot reassure someone out of avoidance.
You cannot love someone into emotional safety.

An avoidant must:

- acknowledge their pattern
- want to grow
- want to communicate
- want connection more than safety

Otherwise, ghosting will remain their default exit.

8. The Hard Truth: Ghosting by an Avoidant Is Not About You

Read this carefully:

When an avoidant ghosts, it's not because you weren't enough.
It's because **emotional closeness was too much** for them.

Your value did not decrease.
Their emotional capacity was simply limited.

And ghosting became their escape.

CLOSING THOUGHT FOR CHAPTER 7

Avoidants aren't evil —
they're overwhelmed.

Ghosting is the reflection of **their limits**, not your desirability.

And understanding this frees you from taking the disappearance personally.

CHAPTER 8

THE NUANCES THAT LEAD TO GHOSTING**

BY PHIL TURNER JR.

Ghosting rarely comes from one big moment.

It usually comes from **a cluster of small, subtle, deeply human interactions** that reveal compatibility—or the lack of it.

These nuances matter because relationships live or die in the space between intention and interpretation.

This chapter covers the things people rarely talk about... the stuff that *actually* makes someone pull back, shut down, or disappear.

Not every item will apply to you.

But enough of them apply to enough people that ignoring them is risky.

Let's get into it.

1. Being "Too Ghetto, Too Aggressive, Too Confrontational"

(Clarified, not racial — strictly behavioral)

"Ghetto" in this book refers to **behavior**, not race, culture, or socioeconomic background.

It means:

- Loud arguments in public
- Cursing at staff, servers, or strangers
- Starting confrontations to "prove a point"
- Throwing shade at other women for no reason

- Speaking unfiltered without considering the environment
- Being quick to escalate instead of de-escalate

These behaviors trigger a danger response in men **and women**.

Nobody wants a partner who might embarrass them in public or create unnecessary conflict.

People ghost to protect their peace.

2. Freeloading Friends

A partner pays attention to the company you keep.

If your friends:

- Always need a ride
- Always need to borrow money
- Always need you to "hold them down"
- Drain your time
- Bring drama
- Constantly need rescuing
- Interfere in your relationships

…a serious person will distance themselves.

You don't have to cut friends off, but you *do* need boundaries. If you can't enforce boundaries, the person you're dating will ghost before that "friend" becomes **their** responsibility.

3. Meddling Friends

Some women have "council of girlfriends."
Some men have "the fellas."
Either one can destroy a relationship fast.

- Friends who ask inappropriate questions
- Friends who compare your partner to their partner
- Friends who push you toward breakups
- Friends who don't want to lose access to you
- Friends who project their bitterness

Meddling = relationship death.

If the person you're dating sees your friends controlling your decisions, they'll ghost because:

They don't want a relationship with a committee.

4. Being Easy—or Hard—on His Wallet

Money is emotionally loaded.
Two things make men ghost FAST:

(1) A woman who treats his money like her right
Demands, suggestions, "You should take me here,"
or being offended at a budget-friendly date.

(2) A woman who refuses to be considerate of his wallet

Not understanding:

- Gas prices
- Commute time
- Child support
- Medical bills
- Inflation
- Business slow seasons

People ghost when they feel like they can't win financially.

A woman who's *mindful* of a man's wallet is rare—and deeply appreciated.

5. When a Woman Makes More Money (And Thinks He's Intimidated)

This one creates ghosting on both sides.

Many women assume:

"He must be intimidated by my success."

Sometimes that's true.
But often:

- She becomes condescending
- She talks to him like an intern
- She stops receiving
- She believes she's the "prize" and he's lucky
- She throws subtle jabs

- She treats him like a project

So he ghosts.

Not because of her income—but because of her **energy**.

Projection destroys chemistry.

6. Vague Explanations

One of the top ghosting triggers:

"I'm going through some things right now."
"I just need to figure life out."
"It's complicated."

Adults crave clarity.
Ambiguity feels manipulative.

When your communication lacks specificity, people assume:

- You're hiding someone
- You're juggling options
- You're emotionally unavailable
- You lack self-awareness
- You're not serious

Ghosting is their way of opting out quietly.

7. "He's Not Your Girlfriend—She's Not Your Bro"

Men and women process differently.

Men: direct, brief, solution-oriented.
Women: detailed, expressive, connective.

Problems happen when:

- You overshare with him like he's your girlfriend
- You under-communicate with her like she's one of the guys

People ghost when:

- The conversations are draining
- The emotional labor is too heavy
- The tone feels disrespectful
- The vibe feels mismatched

Communication style compatibility is more important than most realize.

8. Grown Kids Living at Home

This is delicate—but real.

It's not the *kids* that trigger ghosting.
It's the **dynamic**:

- No discipline
- No structure

- No work ethic
- Entitlement
- Adult sons acting like they're "the man of the house"
- Disrespect toward the dating partner
- Sneakiness
- Tension and testosterone in the home
- A woman choosing the child over EVERY boundary

Today's economy keeps young adults home longer. That's not the issue.

The issue is when:

They don't WANT to move out — and you enable it.

People ghost when they can see they'll never have a peaceful home with you.

9. Divorce Dynamics

Divorce changes everything—especially with kids.

The biggest ghosting triggers:

- Court schedules
- Switching weekends
- Money disputes
- Constant disagreements with an ex
- Emotional residue

- Loyalty binds
- Kids weaponized
- Holidays and pockets of emotional triggers

Here's the truth:

Most people today don't ghost the *person*—they ghost the **system surrounding that person.**

If your life looks chaotic, they'll avoid joining the chaos.

10. The Double-Bind Parenting Trap

(*When he has kids — and the new partner makes it harder*)

This is a ghosting situation that men rarely talk about publicly.

Here's the setup:

- His ex calls because something is broken in the house
- Money is tight
- The kids need something
- He feels obligated to help
- His new partner gets irritated, jealous, or resentful
- He feels like he's failing as a father AND as a man to his new partner

So he ghosts.

Not because he didn't care…

…but because he could not win without hurting someone.

Yes, this works both ways — women face it too.
We'll cover the female version shortly.

11. Bad Sex (The Elephant in the Room)

Nobody wants to say it.
Everyone feels it.

Bad sex is a major cause of ghosting because sexual compatibility is not optional.

Bad sex includes:

- No rhythm
- No awareness
- No feedback
- No enthusiasm
- Mechanical movements
- Inhibition
- Overconfidence
- Roughness with no consent
- Assuming what ex-lovers loved must work on everyone
- Squeezing down too hard ("gripping")
- Aggressive nipple play

- Biting ears when someone hates it
- Neck kissing that actually irritates
- Oral sex that's painful
- Being too timid or too porn-scripted

Sex is personal.
Ghosting is the exit when sexual compatibility feels hopeless.

12. Mismatched Sexual Expectations

Many women want to know a man is serious before intimacy.
Healthy.

But here's an uncomfortable truth:

A man cannot know he wants a future until he knows he enjoys the sex.

Women fall in love → then desire grows.
Men desire → then fall in love.

If the sex is:

- Awkward
- Emotionally stiff
- Too slow
- Too fast
- Too routine
- Too transactional

He may not ghost immediately…
but his energy will decline.

This isn't superficial — it's neurological, biological, and real.

13. Sexual Frequency

People have different frequencies:

- Daily
- Several times a week
- Once a week
- Twice a month
- Rarely

Mismatch causes frustration.

Sexually frustrated people ghost—or cheat—or become resentful.

Sex frequency must be communicated early.

14. Pre-Sex Conversations That Prevent Ghosting

Before things get physical, both should ask:

- *What turns you on?*
- *What turns you off?*
- *Is there anything painful or off-limits?*
- *Do you prefer slow or intense?*

- *Are nipples sensitive?*
- *Do you like oral? Giving? Receiving?*
- *Anything to avoid?*
- *How important is frequency?*

These conversations remove awkwardness and prevent misunderstandings that lead to someone disappearing.

15. Oversharing to Strangers

Some people talk too much, too soon, too deeply.

When someone overshares:

- Trauma
- Secrets
- Family dirt
- Finances
- Sexual history
- Mental health details
- Personal issues of friends
- Work gossip
- Court cases

On date one or two…

The listener thinks:

"If you tell me all this now, what will you reveal later?"

People ghost when they can't trust your mouth.

16. Guarded Behavior

This was covered earlier, but deserves emphasis here:

- Guarded at first
- Loving after sex
- Then clingy
- Then anxious
- Then accusatory
- Then fearful
- Then projecting past hurts

This emotional swing scares people.

Ghosting becomes self-protection.

17. After-Sex Behavior

Two people can have great chemistry...
then sex changes everything.

Men often withdraw because testosterone dips after release.

Women often increase closeness because oxytocin rises.

But ghosting happens when:

- She becomes accusatory
- He becomes emotionally distant
- She interprets his sleepiness as rejection
- He interprets her needs as pressure

- Either side becomes insecure

Sex doesn't fix dynamics — it reveals them.

18. The Godly Man Paradigm

Still one of the biggest ghosting triggers among believers:

- Unclear spiritual expectations
- Misused scripture
- Religious shaming
- Deeming someone "unequally yoked" without definition
- Talking religion but not living it
- Treating church rules like dating rules
- Wanting a spiritual leader while resisting leadership
- Claiming "God told me" as conflict avoidance
- Using spirituality to hide emotional immaturity

Ghosting occurs because:

People want clarity—not spiritual jargon.

If you can't explain your spiritual standards plainly, you will unintentionally push away good people.

19. First Date Attire

People judge—period.

Not unfairly.

Just honestly.

Men and women ghost based on:

- Overly sexy
- Too conservative
- Too bougie
- Too flashy
- Too sloppy
- Too revealing
- Too masculine or too feminine in presentation
- Heavy perfume
- Loud makeup
- Poor grooming
- Hair unkept
- Nails dirty
- Clothes smelling stale

Appearance communicates values before words ever do.

20. Exaggerations That Feel Like Lies

You don't need to lie to ruin trust—
exaggeration does it for you.

People ghost when they detect:

- Embellished stories
- Inflated accomplishments
- Slight inconsistencies
- Humble brags

- Resume-style dating
- Overstated trauma
- "Everyone wants me" energy

Authenticity beats performance every time.

21. Politics & Hot-Topic Issues

You can like someone…
until their worldview hits you in the face.

Issues that instantly cause ghosting:

- Sexual identity views
- Abortion
- Political parties
- Conspiracy beliefs
- Religion
- Parenting styles
- Vaccines
- Racial tensions
- Gender wars
- Social justice debates

People ghost because they know:

"We'll never agree, and I don't want to fight about it."

Compatibility is not just emotional—it's ideological.

22. Moms With Young Kids

Single moms and solo moms often date successfully. But ghosting happens when:

- The schedule is unpredictable
- Discipline is inconsistent
- The father creates chaos
- Babysitters fall through
- Kids interrupt every date
- The man is expected to immediately help financially
- She uses her kids as an excuse
- There is no balance
- Kids are overly entitled
- The man feels like a replacement dad too soon

Some men ghost because they don't want conflict with kids or exes.

Some women ghost because they fear introducing a man too soon.

Both sides need gentleness and patience.

23. Bro Pressure (Male Version)

Men lose good women because of the fellas.

Why men ghost due to bro pressure:

- Friends who clown him for being in love
- Friends who encourage cheating
- Friends who call his woman "too much"
- Friends who say he's "whipped"
- Friends who push him back into the streets
- Friends who feel threatened by his stability
- Friends who don't want to lose him

If a man is emotionally immature, he lets outside approval override his own desires.

Ghosting becomes the path of least resistance.

24. Jealous Friends

Story 1: Tasha & Marcus

Tasha finally met a good man — responsible, attentive, solid.
Her friend group wasn't used to seeing her with a man of that caliber.

- They questioned his motives
- Whispered insecurities into her ear
- Compared him to "their type"

- Told her he was out of her league
- Suggested he was a player
- Made jokes about him being "too good to be true"

Tasha shifted her behavior.

Marcus felt the change immediately.

He didn't argue.

He simply slid out of the situation.

Ghosted — not because of her…
but because of her **circle**.

Story 2: Michelle & Ray

Michelle introduced Ray to her friends at brunch.

They were cool until Ray paid the bill without hesitation.

Suddenly:

- They assumed he was a trick
- They implied she should "level up her demands"
- They pressured her to ask for more
- They compared their own men negatively

Michelle let their voices override her own feelings.

Ray went quiet… then gone.

Story 3: Erica & Devon

Erica's friends were single and angry about it.

When she met Devon — consistent, honest, stable —
they did everything to sabotage it:

- Convincing her he was too boring
- Telling her she "deserved more"
- Making fun of his job
- Picking apart his clothes
- Calling him "average"

Devon felt judged and unwelcome.
He didn't argue.
He didn't compete.

He ghosted.

Not because of Erica — but because he refused to date *her entire committee*.

25. Life Pace Mismatch

Some people move fast.
Some people move slow.
Some are planners.
Some are spontaneous.
Some live by routine.
Some live by flow.

Ghosting happens when:

- One person is future-minded and the other isn't
- One wants stability and the other wants freedom
- One prioritizes peace and the other prioritizes excitement

- One is wired for family and the other for independence

Life pace determines relationship peace.

26. Behavior Around Your Ex

People ghost when they see:

- You still argue with your ex
- You still do favors
- You still respond emotionally
- You still complain daily
- You still follow their social media
- You still bring their name up
- You still seem attached
- You let them disrespect your boundaries

Ghosting is simply:

"I don't want to step into your unresolved story."

27. Social Media Personality vs Real-Life Personality

Some people ghost because:

- You're peaceful in person but chaotic online
- You post thirst traps
- You post negativity

- You share quotes attacking men or women
- You overshare your business
- You subtweet
- You live in comments sections
- You create content instead of connection

Ghosting is often a quiet statement:
"I don't want my life connected to your online identity."

28. Emotional Negotiation

People ghost when:

- Everything turns into a debate
- Everything feels like a negotiation
- They can't express a need without a counterargument
- They feel interrogated
- They feel judged
- They feel misunderstood
- They feel unsafe emotionally

Emotional freedom is oxygen.
Without it, people leave.

29. Lack of Accountability

Ghosting often happens when someone notices:

- Every conflict is someone else's fault
- You never apologize

- You minimize hurtful behavior
- You justify disrespect
- You explain instead of reflect
- You can't say "I was wrong"
- You weaponize your trauma

Emotionally mature people don't stay where account-ability is absent.

30. No Mystery, No Depth

Oversharing, constant posting, needing validation, trauma dumping...

All create a lack of mystery.

People ghost when:

They feel like they met every version of you in one week.

Mystery creates attraction.
Not secrecy — but pacing.

31. Hygiene & Personal Habits

(You requested specifics)

- Bad breath
- Body odor
- Dirty ears
- Messy nails

- Visible buildup on teeth
- Clothes that smell like mildew
- Food left on the mouth
- Chewing loudly
- Blowing nose at the table
- Farting casually
- Hair shedding everywhere
- Excessive perfume or cologne

People do not ghost because they are mean.
They ghost because attraction is sensory.

32. Porn Script vs Real-World Sex

This needed its own section.

Some people "perform" instead of connect.

Ghosting happens when:

- Sex feels like a reenactment
- Movements are unnatural
- Everything feels staged
- There's no emotional presence
- The other person feels like a prop
- Consent is assumed instead of requested
- Everything is too aggressive
- The person tries every trick on day one

People want erotic connection, not a performance showcase.

33. When Someone Says "You're Insecure"

You requested this section.

This phrase is often weaponized.

Sometimes:

- It's projection
- It's dismissive
- It avoids accountability
- It's used to shame a valid concern
- It shuts down communication
- It makes someone doubt their own instincts

When someone repeatedly calls you "insecure" rather than addressing your concern, ghosting becomes self-protection.

NOTE: When Someone Ghosts Because of a Sexual Health Issue (Herpes, HPV, HIV, etc.)

This is one of the most sensitive — and most misunderstood — reasons people disappear.
And although the world is more educated today about STIs, the emotional fear has not caught up with the medical facts.

Many people don't ghost because they're dishonest or manipulative.
They ghost because they are terrified.

Terrified of:

- **rejection**
- **judgment**
- **humiliation**
- **being labeled "dirty," "careless," or "unsafe"**
- **having their private medical history shared**
- **ruining a connection they were actually excited about**

And the most common STI behind "disappearing behavior" — the one I've seen most in coaching — is **herpes (HSV-1 and HSV-2).**

Not because it's the most dangerous.
But because it's the most *stigmatized*.

What really happens internally

When someone develops feelings for a new person, the anxiety can become overwhelming:

- "How do I tell them?"
- "What if they reject me immediately?"
- "What if this ruins everything?"
- "What if they think I'm irresponsible?"
- "What if they tell someone else?"
- "What if they think my entire character is based on a virus?"

The pressure builds so high that **disappearing feels safer than explaining**.

For some people, ghosting becomes an emotional escape hatch.

They don't want to lie.
They don't want to lead anyone on.
But they also don't feel safe telling the truth.

So they disappear.

Real story

A woman I once coached had gone on three amazing dates with a man who genuinely liked her.
But the night before he invited her over for dinner, she panicked.
She had HSV-2 and had not told him yet.
Her last disclosure resulted in a man calling her "reckless," so this time she froze.

Her exact words to me were:

"I liked him too much to tell him… and I liked him too much to sleep with him without telling. So I just disappeared. I couldn't handle either option."

She didn't ghost because she was careless or insincere.
She ghosted because her shame was louder than her hope.

That is more common than most people know.

What the other person usually feels

- Confused
- Rejected
- Blindsided
- Wondering what they "did wrong"
- Assuming the attraction just wasn't mutual

Meanwhile, the person who ghosted is often silently grieving the connection but cannot overcome the fear of disclosure.

Why this matters in a book about ghosting

Because **not all ghosting is selfishness.**
Some ghosting is **self-protection** rooted in trauma, stigma, fear, or past cruelty.

If we don't talk about this, we leave out one of the biggest unspoken reasons for sudden disappearances.

Advice for anyone struggling with disclosure

1. **Know the facts:**
2. Herpes, HPV, and many STIs are medically manageable — some extremely common.
3. They are not character flaws.
4. **Plan your disclosure:**
   - o Choose a calm moment.
   - o Speak confidently, without shame.
   - o Share the facts, not the fear.

5. **Lead with humanity, not apology:**
6. "I value honesty and safety. I also value this connection, so there's something important I want to share…"
7. **Give the other person space to respond:**
8. Their reaction does not define your worth.
9. **Understand this truth:**
10. The right person can handle reality.
11. **Do not disclose too early or too late:**
12. Before intimacy — always.
13. But only after emotional safety has been established.

Why some people still ghost even after learning all this

Because fear doesn't disappear just because information is available.

Shame is a deeper wound.

Ghosting, in these cases, is not about rejecting the other person —
it's about not wanting to be rejected *because of something that doesn't define them.*

Closing Summary of Chapter 9

Ghosting is almost never about:

- Looks
- Age

- Income
- Education
- Status

It's about:

- Emotional safety
- Peace
- Compatibility
- Personal behavior
- Environment
- Expectations
- Values
- Communication
- Timing
- Maturity
- Fear

Once you understand these nuances, dating becomes less confusing and much more predictable.

CHAPTER 9

THE CHECKLIST: SELF-AWARENESS, ATTRACTION, AND GHOST-PROOFING YOURSELF**

You can't control who ghosts you.

You *can* control what you present, how you connect, and whether someone feels safe building something with you.

This chapter gives you the ultimate **ghost-proofing checklist**—not to make you perfect, but to make you *aware*.

Awareness eliminates confusion.
Awareness eliminates overthinking.
Awareness eliminates "Why did they disappear?"

Let's walk through the areas that matter most.

1. Emotional Readiness Checklist

Before dating anyone, ask yourself:

✓ Am I actually available?

Not lonely…
Not bored…
Not healing from someone else…
Available.

✓ Am I emotionally consistent?

Ghosting often happens because someone senses emotional volatility.

✓ Do I know my needs without demanding them?

Adults can articulate, not manipulate.

✓ Am I still comparing this person to my ex?

If you're still arguing with someone in your past, you're not present.

✓ Do I communicate interest without smothering?

Interest is attractive.
Neediness is not.

If you can't check these boxes, ghosting becomes predictable.

2. Communication Checklist

Most ghosting happens here.

✓ Can I speak directly without being harsh?

People run from communication that feels like conflict.

✓ Can I give clarity when needed?

Vague people get ghosted.

✓ Am I overtalking or undertalking?

- Too many words = emotional overflow.
- Too few words = emotional starvation.

✓ Do I assume or ask?

People run from mind readers.

✓ Am I texting like I'm talking to a friend or an adult?

Tone matters.

If communication with you feels draining, confusing, heavy, or unsafe…
disconnection happens fast.

3. Attraction Energy Checklist

This has nothing to do with beauty.
Attraction energy is:

✓ How you carry yourself

Posture, confidence, warmth.

✓ How you show interest

Subtle signals, not pressure.

✓ How you pace the connection

Not rushing.
Not stalling.
Just right.

✓ **How you make someone feel**

People remember the feeling more than the facts.

✓ **Whether you bring calm or chaos**

Peace is today's #1 currency.

Ghosting is often a reaction to energy, not appearance.

4. Life Stability Checklist

A person doesn't need perfection—but they do need **predictability**.

✓ **Are my finances stable enough for dating?**

Not wealthy—just not drowning.

✓ **Is my schedule manageable?**
✓ **Are my friendships healthy?**

(Or are they jealous, messy, draining?)

✓ **Is my living environment peaceful?**

✓ **Do I have independent hobbies, interests, and identity?**

People ghost chaos.
They stay for stability.

5. Lifestyle & Values Alignment Checklist

People don't ghost because of difference.
They ghost because of **misalignment**.

✓ **Do we share similar views on relationships and commitment?**

If one is serious and the other is slow-walking, ghosting often fills the gap.

✓ **Are our morals, ethics, and lifestyles compatible?**

✓ **Do our views on children, family, faith, and money align?**

✓ **Do we both value peace? Or does one person thrive on drama?**

People withdraw when the differences feel unbridgeable.

6. Sexual Compatibility Checklist

Most people won't say it—but sex either strengthens connection or kills it.

✓ **Do we communicate sexual boundaries and preferences?**

✓ **Do we respect how the other person's body works?**

✓ **Do we have honest conversations before intimacy?**

✓ **Are we aligned on sexual frequency?**

✓ **Are we comfortable giving feedback without hurting each other?**

Sexual frustration, mismatch, or awkwardness causes ghosting more than anything else in dating — and most people never admit it.

7. Behavior, Maturity & Presentation Checklist

The small things are actually the big things.

✓ **Am I well-groomed?**

Clean breath, clean nails, clean clothes.

✓ **Do I overreact to minor things?**

✓ **Am I kind to service workers?**

✓ **Do I speak respectfully in public?**

✓ **Do I avoid gossip and oversharing?**

✓ **Do I manage my emotions without making a scene?**

Maturity is attractive.
Immaturity is loud.

8. Vulnerability & Safety Checklist

People ghost when something feels unsafe.

✓ **Can I be vulnerable without trauma dumping?**

✓ **Do I give others emotional room to breathe?**

✓ **Do I accept "no," "not yet," or "I need time" without spiraling?**

✓ **Do I create a space where someone feels they can be honest?**

✓ **Do I hear what's said, not what I fear?**

When people feel emotionally safe with you, ghosting becomes rare.

9. Exes, Co-Parents & Past Attachments Checklist

People don't ghost the relationship.
They ghost the *baggage*.

✓ **Am I still emotionally connected to an ex?**

✓ **Are there unresolved fights, money issues, or jealousy with an ex?**

✓ **Does co-parenting create drama?**

✓ **Are my past wounds healed enough to not project?**

If your past still has a grip, the present cannot hold you.

10. Standards, Boundaries & Self-Respect Checklist

Ghosting often happens when someone senses:

- No boundaries
- No backbone
- No standards
- No structure
- No consequences

Ask yourself:

✓ **Do I set boundaries without being controlling?**

✓ **Do I communicate expectations respectfully?**

✓ **Do I walk away from disrespect?**

✓ **Do I know what I want and need, clearly?**

✓ **Do I hold myself accountable the same way I hold others?**

People ghost those who don't respect themselves—because the relationship becomes too unpredictable.

11. Social Circle & Outside Influence Checklist

Your village can sabotage your future without meaning to.

✓ **Are my friends supportive or jealous?**

✓ Do they influence my decisions too much?

✓ Do they compare, criticize, or create doubt?

✓ Do they keep me single so they won't be alone?

✓ Do I have the courage to choose my own path?

People ghost when they see your friends are the real decision-makers.

12. Expectations & Pace Checklist

Ghosting often follows mismatched timing.

✓ Am I expecting too much too soon?

✓ Am I expecting too little and giving mixed signals?

✓ Do I escalate emotional talk too quickly?

✓ Do I create pressure without realizing it?

✓ Do I expect a relationship before trust?

No one wants to feel rushed, trapped, or smothered.

13. Personal Integrity Checklist

This is where long-term compatibility lives.

✓ Do I say what I mean?

✓ **Do I show up consistently?**

✓ **Do my actions match my words?**

✓ **Do I respect time, commitments, and promises?**

✓ **Am I honest about my intentions?**

Ghosting happens when trust cracks — even slightly.

14. Self-Audit: "Would I Date Me?"

This is the most important question in the entire book.
Not:

- *Am I attractive?*
- *Do I deserve love?*
- *Am I a good person?*

But simply:

**"If I met someone who acted, communicated, and behaved exactly like me…
would I want to stay, or would I ghost?"**

That question alone reveals everything.

15. The Power of Choosing Yourself First

This checklist is not about perfection.
It's about *awareness*.

Ghosting hurts.
But understanding it protects you.

When you become:

- Balanced
- Emotionally healthy
- Clear
- Secure
- Attractive from the inside out
- Consistent
- Peace-oriented

…you naturally reduce the chances of someone disappearing.

You can't force someone to stay.
But you can make yourself the kind of person someone **wouldn't want to lose**.

And that is how you ghost-proof your future.

CHAPTER 10

THE TRUTH ABOUT CONNECTION

BY PHIL TURNER JR.

Men, Women & How They Bond Differently

Most people think connection looks the same on everyone. It doesn't. Men and women *bond*, but they bond differently — and misunderstanding that difference is where a lot of confusion starts.

Many men connect through presence, time spent, and the feeling of "I'm here with you."
Many women connect through emotional safety, consistency, and how a man handles the parts of her she doesn't show the world.

Neither style is wrong.
But when you don't understand each other's pace or wiring, you'll misread timing, silence, and intention. That's usually where the disconnect happens. Some call it ghosting — often, it's just two people bonding on different timelines.

Connection works when you stop expecting someone to love you the way *you* love, and start learning the way *they* do.

Emotional Safety — The Real Glue of Relationships

Chemistry is easy.
Conversation is fun.
But emotional safety? That's what makes someone stay.

Emotional safety shows up when:
- You can speak without being judged
- Your vulnerability isn't used against you
- You don't have to rehearse every sentence
- You feel understood, not just listened to

Most people aren't pulling away because they don't like you. They pull away because they don't feel *safe* being who they are around you — or they haven't developed the courage to be emotionally honest.

Emotional safety is the quiet force behind commitment. Without it, everything else is temporary.

Why Some People Will Never Give Closure

People love to demand closure, but they rarely admit one truth:
Some individuals simply don't have the emotional capacity to give it.

They avoid closure because it forces them to be accountable. It forces them to explain what they don't want to confront. And it exposes their inconsistencies, their fears, or their lack of maturity.

Some don't give closure because:

- They don't want to be the bad guy
- They fear emotional confrontation

- They don't know how to express themselves
- They're ashamed of how they behaved
- They're still confused themselves

Closure is not what they tell you.
Closure is what you *decide* when their silence tells you everything they wouldn't say.

How to Stop Attracting Ghosting Patterns

Ghosting doesn't come out of nowhere — it follows patterns. And most patterns repeat because we ignore the first sign that tells us something's off.

You break the pattern when you:

- Pay attention to behavior, not promises
- Stop giving deep access to people who earned shallow entry
- Leave at the first sign of emotional instability
- Make peace with "No," "Not ready," or "Not for me"
- Accept that silence is a complete sentence

The cycle stops when your desire for real connection becomes stronger than your tolerance for mixed signals.

What Healthy Connection Actually Looks Like

Healthy connection isn't dramatic. It doesn't require decoding. It doesn't feel like guessing or gambling. Healthy connection feels like two people choosing each other in real time.

It looks like:

- Mutual effort
- Clear communication
- Honesty about feelings and intentions
- Respect for each other's pace
- Accountability when mistakes happen
- Peace — not confusion

Healthy connection feels grounded, steady, and consistent. It doesn't drain you. It doesn't make you question your worth. It makes you breathe easier, not harder.

Anything that constantly makes you anxious is not connection — it's attachment to uncertainty.

**FINAL REMARKS

What Ghosting Really Teaches You — and What to Do Next**

If you've made it this far, it means two things:

1. You're tired of confusion, mixed signals, and emotional guesswork.
2. You're ready to understand relationships on a deeper, more honest level than most people ever will.

Ghosting is painful — not because someone disappeared, but because it leaves a **hole where closure should be**. It makes you question:

- *"Did I do something wrong?"*
- *"Was I not enough?"*
- *"Did I misread everything?"*
- *"Why didn't they just say something?"*

But here's the truth:

Ghosting says far more about the ghoster than it does about you...
yet it still reveals something valuable about *your patterns* too.

And that combination is what this book has been preparing you to see.

Ghosting Isn't About Good or Bad People — It's About Emotional Capacity

Most people don't ghost because they are evil.

They ghost because:

- They are overwhelmed.
- They don't know how to handle conflict.
- They lack relationship skills.
- They can't articulate discomfort.
- They're embarrassed or fearful.
- They sense misalignment and don't know how to say it.
- They want connection without responsibility.
- They're not ready for the version of you they met.
- They cannot give what they know you expect.

Ghosting is a **capacity problem**, not a **character judgment**.

And when you see it through that lens, you stop blaming yourself — and start understanding yourself.

Some Connections End Quietly Because They Were Never Built to Rise

Every person you meet enters your life to show you something:

- What you want.
- What you don't want.
- What you tolerate.
- Where you need healing.
- Where your standards must rise.
- Where your boundaries are too soft or too harsh.
- Where you're repeating patterns you thought you escaped.

No experience is wasted — not even the ones that hurt.

Ghosting is painful.
But it's also directional.
It moves you away from who wasn't meant to stay, and toward someone who will choose you **with clarity, honesty, and consistency**.

What I Want You to Know Moving Forward

Here are the truths I want sealed in your spirit as you put this book down:

1. You are not "too much" — you were simply too much for the wrong person.

The right person will appreciate your depth, your heart, your presence.

2. Ghosting is rejection without confrontation — not rejection of your worth.

Many people don't have the skills to navigate adult conversations.

3. Your value is not reduced because someone failed to recognize it.

Gold is still gold, even in the wrong hands.

4. If someone disappears, believe them.

Don't chase clarity from a person who proved they can't give it.

5. Your emotional safety is your responsibility.

Not their apology.
Not their explanation.
Not their closure.

6. Ghosting stings — but it also saves you.

Imagine the emotional cost of staying attached to someone who lacked honesty from the beginning.

What I Hope This Book Gave You

My mission wasn't to shame anyone.
My mission was to give you **vision**, not just information.

I wanted you to understand the *why* beneath the behavior — the psychology, the patterns, the unspoken rules, the gender differences, the emotional habits, and the nuances that relationships rise or fall on.

I wanted you to see:

- What causes fear
- What creates attraction
- What pushes people away
- What builds emotional safety
- What destroys connection
- And what inspires someone to stay — willingly, not forcefully

I wanted you to have the clarity that most people never receive.

Because when you understand these dynamics, you stop personalizing everything — and you start *observing*.

Observation is power.

For Those Who Want to Go Deeper

If you're reading this and thinking:

- *"I want to understand myself better."*
- *"I want to stop repeating patterns."*
- *"I want to date smarter."*

- *"I want a partner who is emotionally available and ready."*
- *"I want someone who sees me — and stays."*

…I'm here to help.

I've been studying human behavior, relationships, attraction, communication, and emotional patterns for decades.

As a certified Strategic Interventionist and Relationship Coach, I've guided countless people through confusion, heartbreak, and healing into clarity, confidence, and communication mastery.

If you want personalized coaching, you can visit:

www.philturnerjr.com

and connect with me for one-on-one sessions.

I'll help you navigate:

- Dating patterns
- Emotional blocks
- Ghosting trauma
- Relationship readiness
- Attraction energy
- Communication style
- Boundary-setting
- Self-worth rebuilding
- Long-term compatibility

- And understanding exactly *why* someone pulled away

Your clarity is my mission.

My Final Words to You

Ghosting hurts — but it isn't the ending.
It's the doorway.
A doorway into:

- Better self-awareness
- Stronger emotional intelligence
- Clearer standards
- Healthier attachment
- Greater confidence
- Better relationship decisions
- And more fulfilling connections

You deserve someone who shows up with presence, not confusion.
Consistency, not chaos.
Honesty, not silence.
Commitment, not convenience.
Effort, not excuses.

May you never again internalize someone else's emotional unavailability as a reflection of your worth.

May you become so grounded in who you are that anyone who is not aligned simply fades out — without damaging your peace.

And may this book help you recognize, with confidence:

When someone ghosts you, they did not leave you behind.
They simply removed themselves from a future they weren't equipped to hold.

Your future remains intact.
Your heart remains valuable.
Your capacity for love remains powerful.

And the right person — the one who sees you, chooses you, and stays —
will never have to disappear to prove a point.

**QUICK TIPS

50 Fast Lessons to Prevent Ghosting, Pullbacks, and Confusion**

A rapid-fire summary to reinforce the biggest insights from this book — plus new ones not in earlier editions.

1. "Whatever…" is communication quicksand. It signals frustration, disconnect, or contempt — and most people shut down in response.

2. People connect differently: Many men bond through physical intimacy; many women bond through emotional intimacy.

   Neither is wrong — just understand the wiring.

3. Great sex doesn't equal compatibility……but compatibility becomes very hard when the sex is consistently bad.

4. Confidence, warmth, authenticity, and emotional steadiness are universal attraction magnets — no matter the gender.

5. A person cannot make a lifelong decision about you after a few dates.
   Slow down. Clarity requires time.

6. If you want a high-achieving partner, be a high-achieving counterpart.
    Looks alone aren't a long-term strategy.

7. People ghost over things that seem small to you but feel big to them.

    Don't dismiss another person's emotional triggers.

8. Your partner is not defined by their friends.

    Observe *their* behavior.

9. People stay where they feel understood, appreciated, and emotionally safe.
    Your energy sets the tone.

10. "I trust you" is a powerful signal.
    It inspires most people to rise to it.

11. Achievement-oriented individuals often minimize issues to stay in "solution mode."

    Respect the wiring instead of labeling it "emotionally detached."

12. Don't judge intentions too quickly.
    Most people communicate poorly under pressure.

13. Dating skills ≠ long-term relationship skills.
    Some great partners are terrible initial daters.

14. Be honest about your dating pool.
    Your desired traits should align with what you bring.

15. Extremely attractive people typically have more options.
    Not competition — options.

16. If someone wants exclusivity, they don't want to compete with others you're dating. This applies to all genders.

17. People don't evaluate you through your insecurities.
    They evaluate how you *make them feel*.

18. Don't play "I'll act uninterested so they'll pursue me."
    Healthy adults appreciate clarity, not games.

19. Whatever you highlight grows — negative or positive.
    Focus wisely.

20. If someone asks, "Are you listening?" more than twice, you're not tracking the emotional content.
    Not just the words.

21. Avoid quoting "relationship rules."
    Every human pair has its own ecosystem.

22. Public disrespect — joking or serious — is relationship decay.
    Protect your partner's dignity.

23. Never describe exes in flattering detail.
    People subconsciously compare.

24. Beauty, religion, sex, or good intentions don't keep someone.
    Alignment does.

25. What one person hates, someone else will love.
    Don't generalize one person's preference as gospel.

26. Sexual responsiveness matters to most people.
    Consistency matters more than perfection.

27. Spontaneity strengthens intimacy.
    Not pornography-level spontaneity — simple, real human connection.

28. Clarify interest before sex — without pressure.
    Say what your standards are, not demands.

29. Too many questions make people feel interviewed, not connected.

30. Your children (especially adult children) can create invisible friction.
    Protect the relationship with boundaries.

31. Blended-family expectations must be renegotiated, not inherited.

32. Words without follow-up actions aren't promises — they're performances.

33. Material expectations scare off most partners.
Let generosity flow from desire, not pressure.

34. People want to feel successful in love.
Tell them what makes you feel loved — clearly and calmly.

35. Overly aggressive pursuit signals neediness, not strength.
Let interest breathe.

36. Your partner is not your same-sex best friend.
They communicate differently, bond differently, and process differently.

37. People don't connect dots the same way.
Some think in moments; others think in timelines.

38. If someone says they're fine, respect it.
Silent peace exists.

39. Believe people about major life decisions (kids, marriage, lifestyle).
They usually mean it.

40. Style can evolve. Character cannot.

41. You can't change someone — you can only influence growth through safety.

42. Snooping destroys trust. Once broken, it rarely recovers.

43. People do dumb things and still have good hearts. Pause before judgment.

44. Never brag about gifts from past partners. It screams comparison.

45. Never test loyalty. The test damages the result.

46. Set boundaries without hostility. Firm doesn't require forceful.

47. People don't commit because they love you — they commit when they're *ready* for commitment.

48. Many individuals hide their intentions because they don't want to disappoint or be rejected. Not because they're malicious.

49. Manipulation isn't gender-specific. Both men and women manipulate to get their core needs met — connection, security, validation, attention, or reassurance.

50. Compatibility isn't about perfection — it's about emotional safety, communication ease, aligned values, and consistent effort.

A CLOSING WORD FROM THE AUTHOR

Before you close this book, I want you to breathe for a moment and remind yourself of something important:

- ✓ You are not disposable.
- ✓ You are not forgettable.
- ✓ You are not someone who gets "ghosted" because you lack value.

People disappear for reasons that often have very little to do with you.

Some ghost out of fear. Some out of trauma. Some out of guilt, unhealed wounds, or shame. Some because the connection awakened something they weren't prepared to face. And some because they were never emotionally ready for the type of love you carry.

This book was written to pull back the curtain — to help you understand the patterns, the psychology, the fears, and the quiet truths behind human behavior. Not to judge anyone, but to give you clarity… and peace.

If being ghosted has ever made you question your worth, release that burden now. If someone walked away instead of communicating, let them walk.

The right person doesn't disappear — they show up, consistently.

Thank you for allowing me to speak into your life, your relationships, your healing, and your growth. I've spent decades studying human behavior, relationships, communication, and emotional patterns — and yet, one truth remains the same:

Love is still possible for you. The connection you want is still possible.
And the right person will not run from the depth you bring — they will run *toward* it.

Keep your heart open.
Keep your standards firm.
And keep your spirit soft.

Your story is not over. In many ways… it's just beginning.
— *Phil Turner Jr.*

www.ingramcontent.com/pod-product-compliance
Lightning Source LLC
LaVergne TN
LVHW051348080426
835509LV00020BA/3332